The Musician's Mission

A Chair Yoga Adventure

Written by Maria Oliver

Illustrated by Hannah Marks

About this book

I'm Marv and this is Maya. You're going to come with us on a chair yoga adventure.

Yoga helps our bodies stretch and our minds relax.

When you see text that looks like this, follow the actions to join in with the story. Start here!

Sit up tall with both feet on the floor.

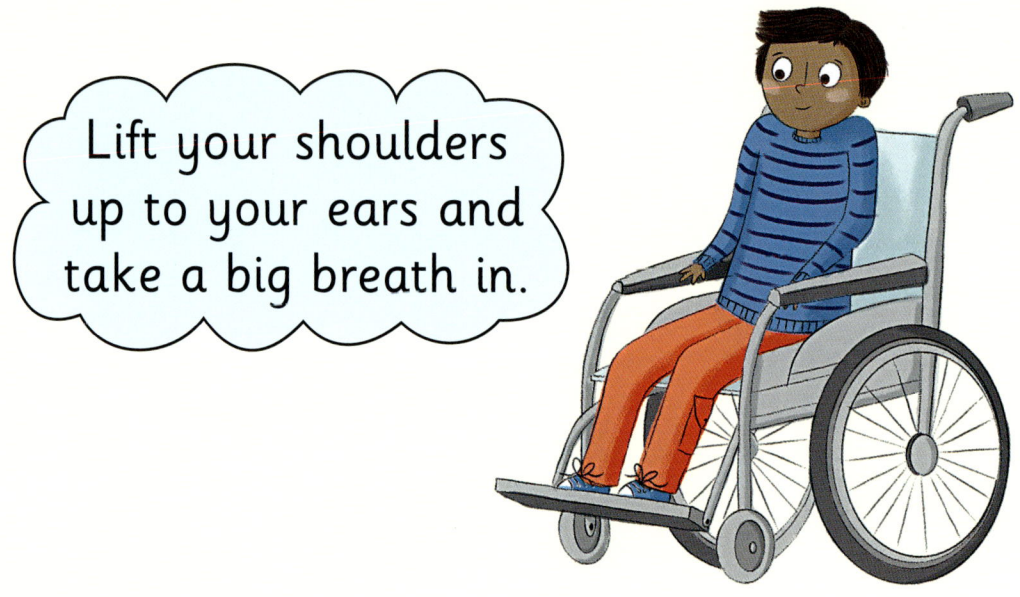

Lift your shoulders up to your ears and take a big breath in.

Now let your shoulders drop back down as you breathe out.

Let's set off on our adventure!

Marv and Maya were on a train. They were meeting Marv's gran at the next station.

The train's rocking motion soon sent them to sleep.

The train whooshed through a tunnel and stopped in a forest.

Pop! Sparkle!

"Did we go in the right direction?" asked Maya.

Sit up to look out of the window.

"Greetings!" said a voice. "My name is Patricia! I called you here using my special flute to help me with a very important mission."

Marv and Maya looked around with confused expressions.

Twist your body right and left to look around.

"I'm looking for four missing animals," said Patricia. "An eagle, a lion, a cobra and a dog need to get back to Swan Lake."

"The animals are hiding after a big storm last night. They won't join us if they don't think we're friendly," said Patricia.

Stretch out your arms and lift one foot for Tree pose.

"I'm sure we can help find the missing animals!" said Marv. "Especially if we show them that yoga makes everyone feel calm."

"I don't think there's another option," agreed Maya.

Walk your feet or wheel your arms forward.

The children followed the magical musician through the forest. Marv told Maya she should copy his yoga movements when they saw an animal.

"Watch out!" cried Maya, as an eagle flew over her head.

Quick! Eagle pose!

Cross your legs and arms, like this.

It worked! The eagle joined their procession in one smooth motion.

Suddenly, a mountain lion ran towards them.

Maya and Marv leaped into action and roared back!

Lean forward, open your eyes and mouth wide, and roar!

Patricia's music seemed to calm the lion, but the roaring noises had attracted some unwanted attention …

"You didn't mention that cobras are so big!" whispered Maya.

"Most snakes are a fraction of this one's size!" said Marv. "Let's stretch while Patricia's music charms it!"

Marv bent forward into the downward-facing dog position.

Something licked Marv's face.

One by one, the animals headed back to their homes.

"Well done for completing your special mission," said Patricia. "As your reward, you'll soon be home, too. Close your eyes …"

Marv and Maya breathed slowly and deeply. As they opened their eyes, they saw Marv's gran walking towards them.

"You look relaxed!" she smiled.

About this book

Try doing the yoga poses again, but if it doesn't feel right, stop!

Your best version of the pose is fine. Don't worry if you don't look exactly like the picture.

Mountain pose

Seated twist

Tree pose

Eagle pose

Lion pose

Cobra pose

Downward-facing dog pose

Use these positions, and your imagination, to create another yoga adventure!

Phonics Practice

Say the sound and read the words.

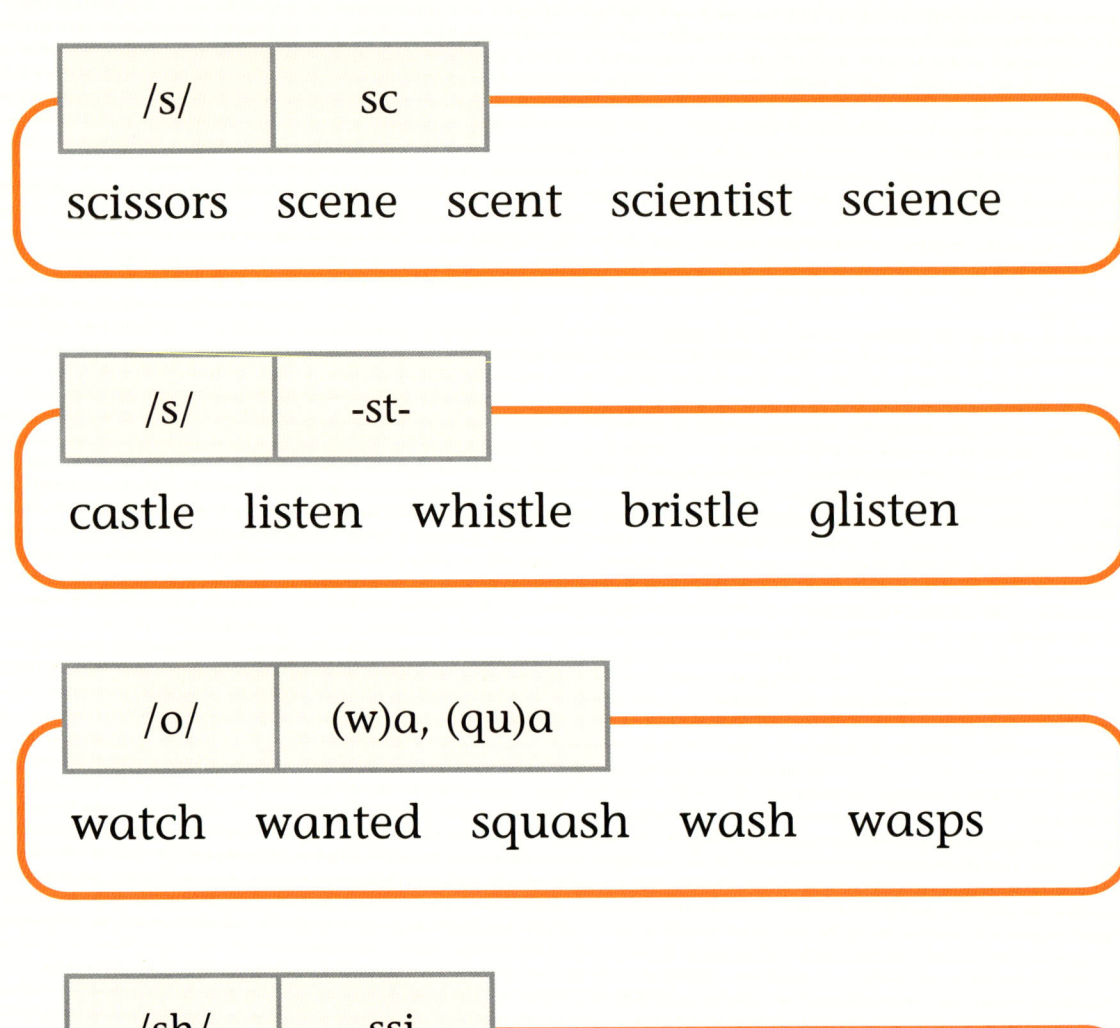

Can you say your own sentences using some of the words on these pages?

What other words do you know that are spelled in these ways?

| /sh/ | -ci |

special   magician   official   social

| /sh/ | -ti |

station   position   mention   imagination

Common exception words

please   oh   their   people   Mr   Mrs

We may say some words differently because of our accent.

Talk about the story

Answer the questions:

1 What made the children fall asleep at the start of the story?

2 Which animal yoga position did the children do first?

3 How did Patricia charm the cobra?

4 How did the children feel before they came home?

5 What helps you to feel relaxed?

6 Which of the yoga positions did you like doing the most, and why?

Can you retell the story in your own words?